W9-AGB-325

CHEMICAL
REACTIONS

by Simon de Pinna
Science curriculum consultant: Suzy Gazlay, M.A.,
science curriculum resource teacher

GARETH**STEVENS**
PUBLISHING
A Member of the WRC Media Family of Companies

Please visit our Web site at: www.garethstevens.com
For a free color catalog describing Gareth Stevens Publishing's
list of high-quality books and multimedia programs, call
1-800-542-2595 (USA) or 1-800-387-3178 (Canada).
Gareth Stevens Publishing's fax: (414) 332-3567.

Library of Congress Cataloging-in-Publication Data

Pinna, Simon de.
  Chemical reactions / Simon de Pinna.
    p. cm. — (Gareth stevens vital science. Physical science)
  Includes bibliographical references and index.
  ISBN-13: 978-0-8368-8084-7 (lib. bdg.)
  ISBN-13: 978-0-8368-8093-9 (softcover)
  1. Chemical reactions. I. Title.
  QD501.P445   2006
  541'.39—dc22   2006033805

This edition first published in 2007 by
Gareth Stevens Publishing
A Member of the WRC Media Family of Companies
330 West Olive Street, Suite 100
Milwaukee, WI 53212 USA

This edition copyright © 2007 by Gareth Stevens, Inc.

Produced by Discovery Books
Editors: Rebecca Hunter, Amy Bauman
Designer: Clare Nicholas
Photo researcher: Rachel Tisdale
Gareth Stevens editorial direction: Mark Sachner
Gareth Stevens editor: Carol Ryback and Leifa Butrick
Gareth Stevens art direction: Tammy West
Gareth Stevens graphic design: Dave Kowalski
Gareth Stevens production: Jessica Yanke and Robert Kraus

Illustrations by Stefan Chabluk
Photo credits: CFW Images: pp. 5 & 14 (Rob Bowden/EASI-Images), 10 (Edward
Parker/EASI-Images); CORBIS: cover; Getty Images: pp. 6 (Hulton Archive), 12 (David
Woodfall), 37 (John Brenneis/Time Life Pictures); Istockphoto: title page, pp. 4
(Michael Smith), 15 (Joe Gough), 17 (Anka Kaczmarzyk), 19 (Alan Goulet), 20, 23
(David Lewis), 24 (Gloria-Leigh Logan), 29 (Steve Allan), 31 (Peter Spiro), 33 (Pulus
Rusyanto), 34 (Peter Guess), 35 (Malcolm Romain), 36 (Shelagh Duffett), 39 (Marco
Regalia), 40 (David Orr), 41 (Mar Stevens), 43 (Kheng Guan Toh); Library of Congress:
p. 21; Science Photo Library: pp. 8 (Andrew Lambert Photography), 27 (Clive
Freeman, The Royal Institution).

Printed in Canada

1 2 3 4 5 6 7 8 9 10 10 09 08 07 06

TABLE OF CONTENTS

Words that appear in the glossary are printed in **boldface** type the first time they occur in the text.

Cover: A beaker of boiling water illustrates a physical change.

Title page: When fireworks light up the night sky, thousands of chemical reactions happen very quickly!

Introduction

It is difficult for people to appreciate the role chemical reactions play in our lives. If you think about chemical reactions at all, you might connect them with terrible smells, newspaper stories about pollution, and tall factory chimneys blowing out clouds of smoke. The fact is that chemical reactions occur a lot more often than that. In fact, many reactions go on around us without us knowing about them!

Many everyday activities involve changing one substance into another. Not all changes are chemical reactions, however. For example, turning liquid water into ice does not involve making a completely new substance. Ice is still the same as water, but it has changed its appearance, or state, as scientists call it. This is an example of a **physical change**. Another example of a physical change is changing liquid water into steam by boiling it. When the steam condenses, it turns back into liquid water. No chemical reaction has happened at all!

If you travel in a car, however, you will probably use gasoline to make it run. Here, the gasoline—which is a **mixture** of substances made from the chemical **elements** carbon and hydrogen—is burned in the engine, together with oxygen, to make new substances such as carbon dioxide. At the same time, energy in the form of heat is released. This process provides power for the car, and the new chemical substances leave the car through the exhaust.

When fireworks light up the night sky, thousands of chemical reactions happen very quickly!

These iron roofs are rusting because they are exposed to oxygen and water.

Your car is probably made of steel, which is a type of iron. If it becomes damaged and isn't immediately repaired, the steel might rust over a period of days or weeks. Rusting is another **chemical change**, requiring oxygen and water, as well as iron, but it is a far slower chemical change than burning fuel.

FISHING FOR SCIENCE

"When I started doing chemistry, I did it the way I fished—for the excitement, the discovery, the adventure, for going after the most elusive catch imaginable in uncharted seas."

Barry Sharpless (b. 1941)
American chemist

Atoms, Molecules, and Compounds

Over two thousand years ago, a Greek thinker named Democritus (c.460–370 B.C.) imagined that if you took a piece of metal foil and cut it in half and then in half again and continued doing so, eventually you would come to the smallest piece of metal possible.

Atoms

Democritus called this smallest possible piece of anything an **atom**, meaning "not cuttable" in Greek. Modern scientists have taken his idea farther. They have evidence from experiments to show that not only is matter made up of atoms, as Democritus

Democritus identified atoms as the smallest building blocks in the universe.

thought, but that even these have smaller parts inside them!

The atoms of nearly all substances contain three sorts of smaller particles: **protons**, **neutrons**, and **electrons**.

Protons

These particles are at the atom's center, in a region called the **nucleus**. The number of protons is unique, like a fingerprint. It tells you from what substance an atom comes. Another feature of protons gives a clue to how **molecules** are constructed and how chemical reactions work. Protons carry a positive electric charge. Because of this, we record them with a "+" sign.

Neutrons

These particles share the nucleus with the protons. They don't have any electrical charge so they are neutral. Neutrons have about the same mass as protons, but their number in the nucleus can vary. For example, some carbon atoms have six neutrons,

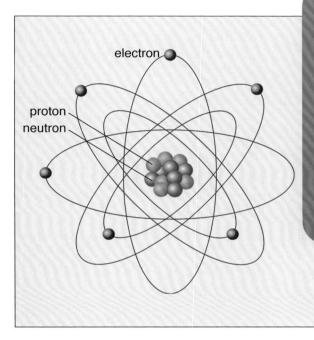

electron

proton

neutron

An atom consists of a nucleus—composed of protons and neutrons—with electrons spinning around it.

some have seven, and others have eight. Despite the different number of neutrons, all three atom examples are still carbon atoms because each of them has six protons.

Electrons

Electrons are the last type of particle in the atom's nucleus. They whirl rapidly around the atom's nucleus, in much the same way as the solar system's planets orbit the Sun.

Electrons are much smaller particles than either protons or neutrons. About 2,000 electrons together have the same mass as a single proton. Electrons have a negative charge. Interestingly, the size of the elec-

tron's negative charge, which can be written with a "–" sign, is equal to the proton's positive charge. This means that a neutral, balanced atom with no overall charge has the same number of electrons as protons.

Molecules

Molecules are made up of atoms. A molecule can consist of all the same atom, or it can be constructed from atoms of different elements. For example, molecules of oxygen or nitrogen gas contain only pairs of oxygen or nitrogen atoms (written as O_2 and N_2). A molecule of carbon dioxide, however, contains one carbon atom and two oxygen atoms—CO_2. A methane molecule consists of one atom of carbon and four atoms of hydrogen—CH_4.

Mixtures and Compounds

The photo below shows two chemicals that are about to take part in a reaction. They are the elements sulfur and iron. Iron is a metal, and sulfur is a nonmetal.

The elements iron (top left) and sulfur (top right) can be combined physically to make a mixture (bottom left). If this mixture is heated strongly, the elements combine chemically to make the compound iron sulfide (bottom right).

When iron filings and sulfur powder are mixed together, we call the chemical combination a mixture. In a mixture, each element retains its original qualities, called properties. This means you could use scientific procedures to separate the iron and the sulfur if you wanted. Can you imagine how you might do that?

But if you heat this mixture, the chemicals actually combine. They create a new substance that looks very different from both iron and sulfur. In this case, the new substance is called iron sulfide. The chemical reaction that has taken place is written as a **formula** like this:

iron + sulfur → iron sulfide

Substances such as iron sulfide, which consist of different elements combined chemically, are called **compounds**. Compounds always have different properties from the elements that make them up. (Note: An arrow, as seen above, is often used in chemical formulas. The arrow suggests that this type of reaction is directional and not reversible.)

Ions

Chemical compounds are not simply collections of different atoms joined together. Under the right conditions, certain atoms taking part in a reaction will lose one or more electrons while others will attract one or more electrons, becoming what are called ions. Ions that have lost electrons are described as positively charged, and ions that have extra electrons are negatively charged.

Common **salt**, for example, is the compound sodium chloride. As the atoms for this compound come together, the sodium atoms lose one electron. Because of the loss, the sodium atoms become sodium ions. Because electrons are electrically negative particles, the loss of the electron makes

the sodium ion less negative than it was. It becomes a "positive" ion, which is written as Na+.

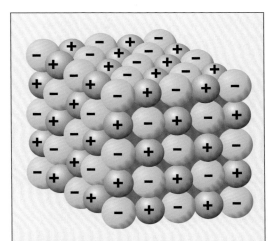

Structure of a crystal of sodium chloride. The positively charged sodium ions (blue) bind with the negatively charged chloride ions (green) to make a cube shape.

The chlorine atom behaves in the opposite way. When it's close to the sodium atom, it takes on an extra electron and becomes more negative than it was—a "negative" ion—and is written as Cl–. When it's an ion, it is called a chloride ion, so the name of the compound becomes "sodium chloride."

Soluble and Insoluble

If salt crystals are mixed with water, they slowly disappear into the water. We say they have dissolved. Substances that dissolve, like salt and sugar, are called **soluble**.

Chemical Reactions

Substances that don't dissolve, such as iron filings or sulfur, are **insoluble**.

When salt and sugar crystals dissolve in water, the particles of salt and sugar have to fit in between the water particles. How easily the particles fit depends on their size.

Separating Mixtures

Mixtures often need to be broken down to obtain pure samples of the substances in them. Different methods can be used to separate the substances within mixtures, depending on whether they are solids mixed with solids, solids with liquids, or even liquids with other liquids. It also depends on whether any of the substances are soluble.

Separating Solids from Liquids

It is usually quite simple to separate an insoluble solid from a liquid by decanting or filtering the mixture.

• *Decanting*: This method involves pouring off the liquid from a vessel that also contains large pieces of a solid substance. Gold prospecting, for example, involves alternately adding water to crushed rock that might contain gold and then swirling it around to separate the lighter impurities from the gold. The impurities can then be decanted off with the water, leaving the heavier gold behind in the pan.

• *Filtering*: This involves pouring a mixture through a piece of material that has small

enough holes to let the liquid but not the solid pieces through it. The filter in a coffeemaker offers an excellent everyday example of how a filter works. It holds back the fine coffee grounds while allowing the hot coffee through.

Separating Solutions

Seawater is a strong solution of water and salt. Take a drink, and you can taste the dissolved salt. How can the salt be separated from sea water?

• *Evaporation*: When seawater is left to dry in the Sun, the heat energy turns the liquid water at the surface into a gas—water vapor. This is **evaporation**. As the water evaporates, it leaves behind white crystals of salt, which can be collected.

These women are gathering salt left by evaporating seawater in the shallow salt lagoons of central Vietnam.

In the same way, in the laboratory, you can boil a solution of any dissolved substance in a glass or ceramic dish to get back the pure substance and evaporate the water.

• *Distillation*: When seawater is heated, the water escapes into the air. What if you wanted to collect the water as well as the salt? You must change the water vapor back into liquid water. This process of changing any vapor back into liquid is called **condensation**.

Distillation is a separation and purification process that removes solids from liquids. It allows you to evaporate the liquid (**solvent**) from the solids (**solute**), catch the vapors, and condense them back into a pure liquid in a separate container from the solids.

In the laboratory, technicians use a device called a condenser to help with the distillation process. The condenser collects the vapor and cools it in a refrigerated pipe that encircles the container holding the vapor. As the vapor temperature drops, it condenses inside a tube and drips down into a receptacle for use. The diagram below shows this process.

Distillation is used to purify water, chemicals, and other products. For example, it is used to obtain pure drinking water from seawater in parts of the Middle East, where water is scarce.

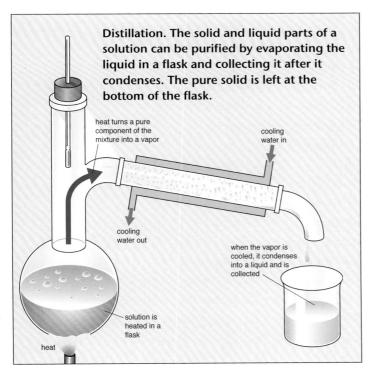

Distillation. The solid and liquid parts of a solution can be purified by evaporating the liquid in a flask and collecting it after it condenses. The pure solid is left at the bottom of the flask.

heat turns a pure component of the mixture into a vapor

cooling water in

cooling water out

when the vapor is cooled, it condenses into a liquid and is collected

solution is heated in a flask

heat

Separating Liquids

If you add oil to water, the two liquids will not mix. Scientists say they are immiscible, which means "unmixable." Such immiscible liquids can be separated by scooping off the top layer or, more completely, by using another piece of lab equipment called a separating funnel. This type of funnel has a **valve** at the bottom, so that you can let the heavier liquid drain through before you close the valve. In that way, you can collect each liquid separately.

But what if the liquids are miscible—that is, what if one

Oil doesn't dissolve in water, so ships use **booms** like this one to contain the oil after an oil tanker spill and remove it before it causes harm to ocean life.

dissolves in the other? Then you have to rely on the liquids having different **boiling points**. This process is called **fractional distillation**. Refineries use fractional distillation to separate a whole range of useful substances, such as gasoline, heating oil, and airplane fuel, from **crude oil**.

When crude oil is distilled in a refinery, high-pressure steam heats the oil mixture to about 1100°Fahrenheit (600°Celsius). As it boils, the vapor rises in a tower-like column and passes through holes punched in a series of trays. The higher it goes, the cooler it becomes. As the temperature of each compound in the vapor drops below its boiling point, it condenses in one of the trays. The liquid is then collected for storage or further processing.

Chromatography

Chromatography is an important technique that can be used to separate mixtures of substances that are similar to each other. For this technique to work, each of the mixture's substances must be slightly more or slightly less soluble than the others in a particular solvent, such as water.

Not only is solubility important in separating substances, but so is color. **Chromatography** means "making colored pictures." The method depends on being able to separate the dissolved substances either because of the chemical differences between solutions of different colors or because of the colors added to them.

For example, take a set of colored felt-tip pens. The ink in these pens is a combination of several chemicals. The chemicals are not quite the same for each pen, because each color uses a different mix of chemicals. You can see this for yourself if you take some strips of filter paper (or paper towels) and put a different-colored spot about one inch (2.5 centimeters) from the end of each strip. Put about 1/2 inch (1–1.5 cm) water in a jar. Drape the strips of paper over the side so that the bottom edge (not the colored spot) touches the water. Watch what happens. The colors that travel faster up the strip are more soluble than the others.

Paper chromatography.
You can find out what colored inks are used to make black ink using a strip of filter paper standing in water.

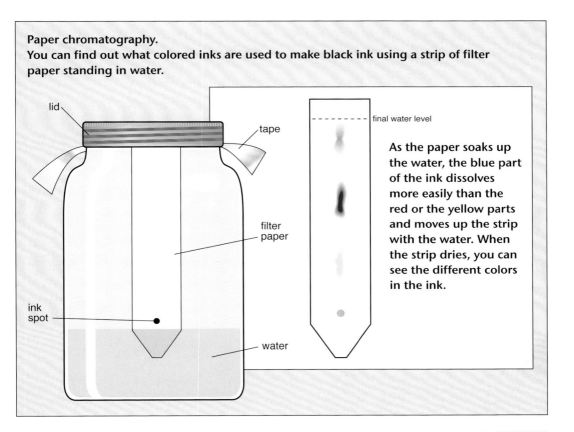

As the paper soaks up the water, the blue part of the ink dissolves more easily than the red or the yellow parts and moves up the strip with the water. When the strip dries, you can see the different colors in the ink.

MARY HEBRAEA—EARLY EGYPTIAN INVENTOR

Mary Hebraea lived in Alexandria, Egypt in the first century A.D. She discovered the formula for hydrochloric acid and invented several pieces of equipment for handling and purifying chemicals. One of her inventions is still known today as the **bain-marie**—the water bath or "double boiler." A double boiler stacks one pan on top of another. Water is boiled in the lower pan to heat the substance in the upper pan. Mary Hebraea also invented a device called the tribikos, which may have been used for distillation.

Did You Know?

DIABETES CHECK
Doctors use chromatography to check samples of urine to see if people have sugar in their urine, which could be a sign of diabetes.

Acids, Bases, and Salts

What are acids and bases? The sharp or sour tastes like that of lemon juice, vinegar, and yogurt, are produced by chemicals known as **acids**. Although many kinds of acids exist, they all have one thing in common— they all contain the element hydrogen. When an acid is dissolved in water, hydrogen is released as positively charged particles, or hydrogen ions. The symbol for a hydrogen ion is H+.

Many acids are described as corrosive, meaning they can dissolve metals such as iron and zinc. Strong acids, such as sulfuric acid, should be treated with care because they give out heat when they dissolve in water, which could cause severe burns. Not all acids are that corrosive, however, and the group, as a whole, has important uses.

Acids are cancelled out, or "neutralized," by substances called **bases** and **alkalis**. A base or an alkali has a bitter taste and feels slippery, like soap. An alkali is a type of base

Oranges, lemons, grapefruit, and limes are all citrus fruits, and all are rich sources of citric acid, one of the most common acids.

Hydrangeas are sensitive to the acidity of the soil. The more acidic the soil, the more blue or purple the flowers will be. Hydrangeas produce pink flowers in less acidic soils.

that dissolves completely in water. Other bases may not dissolve in water. When either an alkali or another base dissolves in a liquid, it releases negatively charged particles. These particles are called hydroxide ions. The hydroxide ion symbol is OH–.

A solution containing a lot of hydroxide ions is considered a strong alkali or strong base, which can burn you just as easily as a strong acid. Strong alkalis are usually found in cleaning products, such as oven cleaner, and are considered **caustic**. Direct contact with caustic chemicals can damage your skin.

Acids and bases are very useful chemicals in industry. For example, they are used in the manufacture of artificial fibers for clothes and in the production of food packaging, paints, and pigments. They are also used as **catalysts** to speed up chemical reactions in the production of medicines and farming chemicals, such as pesticides and herbicides.

Indicators

Although acids and alkalis have particular tastes, many of which you might recognize, tasting a liquid is a dangerous way to find out what it is. A much better way is to use an **indicator**.

Indicators are substances that change color depending on whether they are mixed with an acid or an alkali. Many plant extracts are good indicators—red cabbage juice and black currant juice, for example. The juice of a red cabbage turns from a green color in a strong alkali to blue, purple, pink, and red in a strong acid.

Another plant indicator is called litmus, which is a purple dye that comes from lichens—simple plantlike organisms that grow on trees and rocks. The paper part of litmus strips is made first, soaked in a strong lichen bath, allowed to dry, cut into strips, and packaged. When litmus papers are used, they are dipped and usually read right away, while they are wet. A litmus indicator turns red with acids and blue with alkalis. It is often used in science laboratories, soaked into paper strips and dried.

The pH Scale

Scientists use a special scale to measure the strength of acids and alkalis, called the **pH**

scale. The term pH means "power of hydrogen." The pH scale runs from 0 to 14 and is a measure of the number of hydrogen ions in the solution being measured.

A pH of 0 shows the solution contains lots of hydrogen ions, which indicates a very strong acid. A solution with a pH of 14 contains very few hydrogen ions and is a strong alkali. A solution with a pH of 7 is neither an acid nor an alkali—it is said to be neutral.

pH	Solution is...
0–7	Acidic
7	Neutral
7–14	Alkaline (or basic)

The pH level can be measured more accurately using a piece of sensitive electronic equipment called a pH meter, or it can be measured using a mixture of liquid indicators called a universal indicator. To

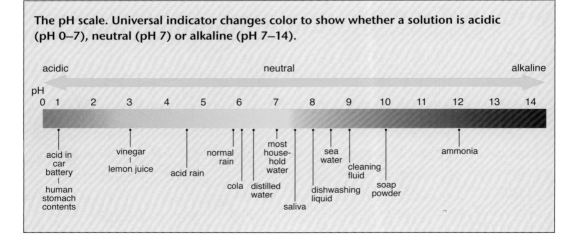

The pH scale. Universal indicator changes color to show whether a solution is acidic (pH 0–7), neutral (pH 7) or alkaline (pH 7–14).

find the pH of a solution, a drop or two of the indicator chemical is added to a sample of the solution. The sample will turn a color according to its pH level. The color is then compared to a range of colors, often displayed on a printed card, to see which color is the closest match.

Acid Precipitation

Normal precipitation is slightly acidic with a pH of about 5.6. Naturally occurring carbon dioxide in the Earth's atmosphere dissolves in water droplets, forming a very weak acid called carbonic acid. When the pH of this precipitation is lower than 5.6, it is called "acid precipitation." It is also sometimes known as "acid rain." Acid precipitation is a problem that affects snow, sleet, and hail as well as rain. It affects the animal and plant life in lakes and streams and damages trees. In addition, it speeds up the decay of buildings, statues, and sculptures that are part of our nation's cultural heritage.

Acid precipitation is the direct result of chemical air pollution. Gases such as sulfur dioxide and various nitrogen oxides are the primary cause of acid rain. These gases come from burning **fossil fuels** such as oil, coal, and gas, mostly in power plants, factories, and the vehicles we drive. Acid precipitation occurs when these gases react in the atmosphere with water, oxygen, and other chemicals to form various acidic compounds. Sunlight makes these reactions

These spruce trees have lost their leaves and died because of acid precipitation.

Chemical Reactions

happen even faster. The result is a mild solution of sulfuric acid, ammonium nitrate, and nitric acid. The wind can blow the chemical compounds that cause acid precipitation across hundreds of miles.

Salts

Salts are compounds that occur naturally, and they are often soluble in water. The salt you put on food—sodium chloride—is only one type of salt. Many other types exist, and some are very useful chemicals. Indigestion medicines, paint pigments, insecticides, and fertilizers are all salts.

Chemically, a molecule of any salt usually contains a positively charged metal part, which comes from a base, and a negatively charged nonmetal part, which comes from an acid. An exception is a salt such as ammonium sulfate, used as a fertilizer. Instead of a metal, its positively charged part is the ammonium ion, which can be written as NH4+, containing one nitrogen and four hydrogen atoms.

Making salts

When an acid reacts with a base, the result is a salt plus water:

acid + base $\rightarrow$ salt + water

Sodium chloride is made when sodium hydroxide reacts with hydrochloric acid. This reaction can be written in words and symbols like this:

sodium hydroxide + hydrochloric acid $\rightarrow$ sodium chloride + water

$NaOH + HCl \rightarrow NaCl + H_2O$

This sort of reaction is called a neutralization reaction because, if the hydrogen ions in the hydrochloric acid solution are equal to the number of hydroxide ions in the sodium hydroxide solution, they will react together to make water molecules when the two solutions are mixed. This will eventually produce a solution with a neutral pH.

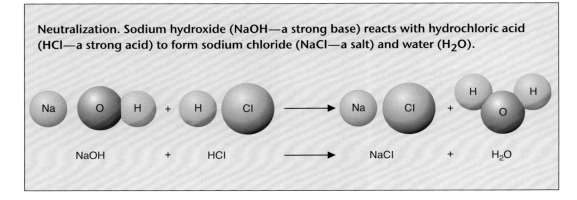

Neutralization. Sodium hydroxide (NaOH—a strong base) reacts with hydrochloric acid (HCl—a strong acid) to form sodium chloride (NaCl—a salt) and water (H_2O).

ACID	SALT NAME	EXAMPLE	USE
Sulfuric acid	Sulfate	Copper sulfate	Wood preservative, fabric dyeing
Hydrochloric acid	Chloride	Sodium chloride	Food additive, water sterilizer
Nitric acid	Nitrate	Potassium nitrate	Fertilizer, gunpowder
Carbonic acid	Carbonate	Calcium carbonate	Building and road construction (as chalk, marble, and limestone)
Citric acid	Citrate	Sodium citrate	Food flavoring and preservative, anticlotting agent in blood bank

Each acid can produce its own family of salts with different bases. The table above shows the salt names for some common acids.

A second way to make a salt is to add a metal directly to an acid:

metal + acid $\rightarrow$ salt + hydrogen

An example would be magnesium, a silvery metal that burns in air with a very bright glow. In hydrochloric acid, magnesium fizzes as it reacts, making bubbles of hydrogen gas and the salt magnesium chloride:

magnesium + hydrochloric acid $\rightarrow$
magnesium chloride + hydrogen

$$Mg + 2\,HCl \rightarrow MgCl_2 + H_2$$

This magnified image shows us the needle-shaped crystals of magnesium sulfate, a salt.

Chemical Reactions

There is a third way to make a salt. Again, it uses an acid, but this time in a reaction with another salt—a carbonate. Acids react with carbonates to produce a salt, water, and carbon dioxide gas.

carbonate + acid $\rightarrow$ salt + water + carbon dioxide

An example would be the reaction between calcium carbonate in the limestone used to construct buildings and sulfuric acid in acid rain:

calcium carbonate + sulfuric acid $\rightarrow$ calcium sulfate + water + carbon dioxide

$$CaCO_3 + H_2SO_4 \rightarrow CaSO_4 + H_2O + CO_2$$

The calcium sulfate does not have the strength of the limestone and crumbles away, weakening the building.

Over many years, acid rain can erode stone figures, such as this church carving.

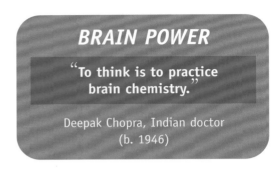

Balancing Equations

When a chemical reaction takes place, atoms rearrange to form products. With this in mind, look again at the symbol equation for the reaction between magnesium and hydrochloric acid. You can see that there is a number in front of the chemical formula for the acid:

$$Mg + 2 HCl \rightarrow MgCl_2 + H_2$$

This equation tells you that there need to be two molecules of acid for every one atom of magnesium for the reaction to work. You can tell that this must be true by counting how many atoms of each element there are in the products of the reaction—the magnesium chloride and the hydrogen gas:

Magnesium:	1 atom
Chlorine:	2 atoms
Hydrogen:	2 atoms

This is what scientists call a "balanced" equation. For an equation to be balanced, you should be able to tell at the end of the

Reaction between a metal and an acid. When magnesium (Mg) metal reacts with hydrochloric acid (2 HCl), the products are magnesium chloride ($MgCl_2$—a salt) and hydrogen gas (H_2).

reaction where all the atoms you started with ended up. There is one atom of magnesium in the salt magnesium, so one molecule of magnesium is all that is required at the start of the reaction.

The only way there could be two atoms of chlorine in the magnesium chloride is if they came from two molecules of hydrochloric acid. For the same reason, two atoms of hydrogen in the molecule of hydrogen gas must also have come from two molecules of the acid.

Law of Conservation of Matter

It was the French scientist Antoine Lavoisier (1743-1794) who first compared how much p luct is made during a reaction ve,   amounts of starting materials, or   From many reactions, Lavoisier   . that, whatever the mass of the   als taking part in a reaction, the   , of the products at the end of the reaction is always the same.

From this, he wrote his law of the conservation of matter, which says that, in a chemical reaction, the "sum of the mass of the reactants equals the sum of the mass of the products."

The French chemist, Antoine Lavoisier.

Chemical Reactions

More Balancing Acts!

Let's look at the neutralization reaction between an alkali and an acid: sodium hydroxide reacting with sulfuric acid. The word equation is:

sodium hydroxide + sulfuric acid → sodium sulfate + water

If we write the chemical formula instead of words, it looks like this:

$$NaOH + H_2SO_4 \rightarrow Na_2SO_4 + H_2O$$

But there's something wrong here! The number of sodium atoms to the left of the arrow doesn't equal the number to the right. There are two atoms of sodium in a molecule of sodium sulfate, and they could only have come from the sodium hydroxide. We could add an extra molecule of sodium hydroxide to rewrite the equation:

$$2\ NaOH + H_2SO_4 \rightarrow Na_2SO_4 + H_2O$$

The number of sodium atoms at the start and at the end of the reaction now balance, but something else has gone wrong. There are now four atoms of hydrogen at the beginning of the reaction—two from the sodium hydroxide and two from the sulfuric acid—but only two at the end, in the water. Likewise, there are six atoms of oxygen in the sodium hydroxide and the sulfuric acid, but only five in the sodium sulfate and the water. Where have the missing atoms gone?

The answer is to double the number of molecules of water produced in the reaction and rewrite the equation so it looks like this:

$$2\ NaOH + H_2SO_4 \rightarrow Na_2SO_4 + 2H_2O$$

Now, if you add up the atoms of each element on the left of the equation, they exactly equal the number of atoms on the right. You must always do this if you want to describe a reaction accurately.

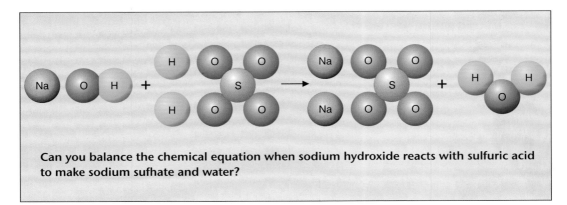

Can you balance the chemical equation when sodium hydroxide reacts with sulfuric acid to make sodium sufhate and water?

SWEET AND SOUR!

Acids in your mouth can dissolve tooth enamel, causing holes where tooth decay can start. These acids are produced by microscopic organisms called bacteria that live in your mouth. Decay is encouraged by sweet foods and drinks, because bacteria grow well on sugars. The waste product they give off is the acid that attacks your teeth.

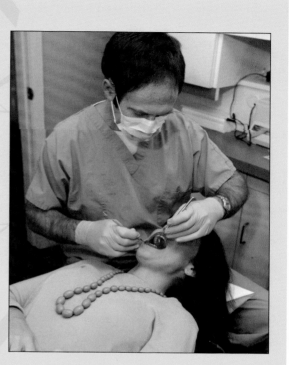

HAROLD HARVEY—FISH BIOLOGIST WHO STUDIED THE EFFECTS OF ACID RAIN

In the 1960s, Canadian Harold Harvey, a biologist from the University of Toronto, studied fish populations in the lakes of northern Ontario (a province of eastern Canada). Harvey found that many species of fish were dying because of increasing acidity of the water.

Painstaking research by Harvey showed that the fish were being killed by acid rain falling on the lakes. The acid rain, he determined, was caused by emissions of sulfur dioxide from coal-fired power plants in the northern United States.

Campaigning by environmental groups eventually led to laws that set controls on gases emitted by power plants. Once that happened, the water quality of lakes in the Ontario region—which includes the Great Lakes—improved, and fish populations began to recover.

CHAPTER 3

Energy and Chemical Reactions

Chemical reactions always involve energy. Energy is needed to make a reaction happen. This amount of energy is called the activation energy. In most cases, the energy is in the form of heat. It could come from the flame of a Bunsen burner, the heat of a match, or the spark between two wires connected to a battery.

A sparkler produces both heat and light when it burns.

Heat Going In — Heat Going Out

Have you ever eaten sherbet? If you have, you will remember how cold your mouth feels after you eat this fruity frozen treat. A chemical reaction occurs in your mouth when the sherbet mixes with your saliva. The warmth of your mouth gives the sherbet enough **activation energy** to start the reaction happening with a chemical in your saliva.

Here's the reaction:

citric acid (from sherbet) + sodium hydrogen carbonate (from saliva) →
sodium citrate + carbon dioxide (the fizz!) + water

As the reaction happens, more and more heat energy is needed to make the molecules of citric acid and sodium hydrogen carbonate react. This energy is taken from your mouth, and so it feels cool compared to the rest of you!

This sort of reaction is called **endothermic**, which literally means "heating the inside," because it needs energy to keep the reaction going. Endothermic reactions absorb heat from the surroundings, and so a beaker containing chemicals reacting endothermically will always feel cold to the touch.

Another endothermic reaction happens when the building material called lime is made by heating limestone:

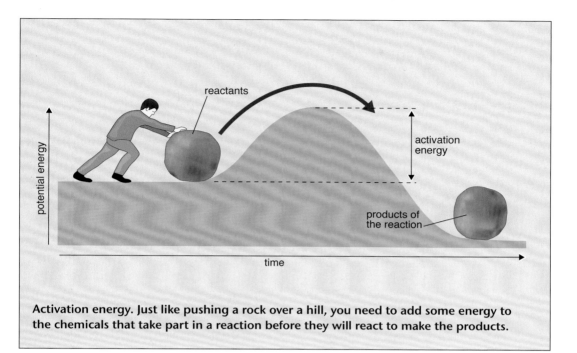

Activation energy. Just like pushing a rock over a hill, you need to add some energy to the chemicals that take part in a reaction before they will react to make the products.

calcium carbonate (limestone) → calcium oxide (quick lime) + carbon dioxide

The calcium oxide is then "slaked" by adding water. This means that water causes the calcium oxide to produce both heat and another form of lime, called slaked lime.

calcium oxide (quick lime) + water → calcium hydroxide (slaked lime) + heat

This time, however, the reaction gives out heat energy. Scientists call reactions that give out energy **exothermic**, which means "heating the outside." Exothermic reactions give out heat and so a beaker containing chemicals reacting exothermically will feel hot if you touch it.

Slaked lime, which is a base, is used by farmers to improve their soil if it is too acidic. Many years ago, builders also used it to make lime mortar before dry cement powder became widely available.

Rearranging Atoms

In every chemical reaction, the links between the atoms in molecules—called bonds—have to be broken before they can be reformed as the new molecules. A bond uses a certain amount of energy to hold two atoms together.

Chemical Reactions

Methane, the main part of natural gas, has a carbon atom joined to four hydrogen atoms by four chemical bonds.

When methane is burned, it reacts with oxygen in the air to form carbon dioxide and water. For this to happen, a certain amount of energy is added—from a burning match, perhaps—to break those four bonds. In other words, breaking chemical bonds is endothermic. The reaction looks like this:

methane + oxygen $\rightarrow$ carbon dioxide + water

$$CH_4 + 2\,O_2 \rightarrow CO_2 + 2\,H_2O$$

But, immediately, even more energy is given out when the atoms join together again to make the products of the reaction, carbon dioxide and water. Making chemical bonds is exothermic.

We've seen that in a chemical reaction, it takes energy to break existing bonds (endothermic) and energy is released when new bonds are formed (exothermic). What about the reaction as a whole? Is it endothermic or exothermic? It depends. If more energy is used to break the bonds than is released when the new bonds form, the overall reaction is endothermic. If more energy is released than was used to break the bonds, the reaction is exothermic. The released energy might be in the form of heat or light or sound. When methane is burned, the overall reaction is exothermic, which is why methane is a valuable fuel for cooking and heating.

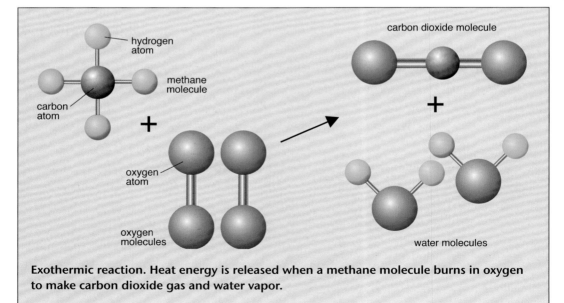

Exothermic reaction. Heat energy is released when a methane molecule burns in oxygen to make carbon dioxide gas and water vapor.

Exothermic Reactions in Living Things

In the cells of your body, glucose sugar from the food you eat reacts exothermically with oxygen that you have breathed in. More energy is released when the products of the reaction are made—carbon dioxide and water—than is needed to break the bonds in the glucose.

glucose + oxygen → carbon dioxide + water

$$C_6H_{12}O_6 + 6\,O_2 \rightarrow 6\,CO_2 + 6\,H_2O$$

The reaction is called respiration, and the energy released is needed to keep your

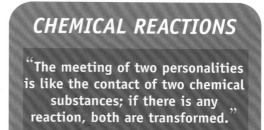

CHEMICAL REACTIONS

"The meeting of two personalities is like the contact of two chemical substances; if there is any reaction, both are transformed."

Carl Gustav Jung, Swiss psychiatrist (1875–1961)

body temperature at 98.6°F (37°C), no matter what the outside conditions. Some of the energy also helps your body move by making your muscles contract to move your skeleton.

Catalysts

Certain chemicals called catalysts can speed up the reaction time simply by being there. They work by lowering the amount of activation energy needed to start a reaction. It is usually the shape of the catalyst molecule, working like a piece in a jigsaw puzzle, that fits with both of the partner molecules in the reaction and holds them together long enough for them to start reacting together. The amazing thing about a catalyst is that it is totally unchanged by the reaction. When the reaction is over, it is exactly the same as it started, which is why you don't see any mention of the catalyst in the equation for the reaction.

A computer-generated view of a zeolite molecule. Zeolite's structure includes miniature channels and tunnels with positive and negative charges. The petroleum industry uses Zeolite as a catalyst for producing different grades of fuels.

Chemical Reactions

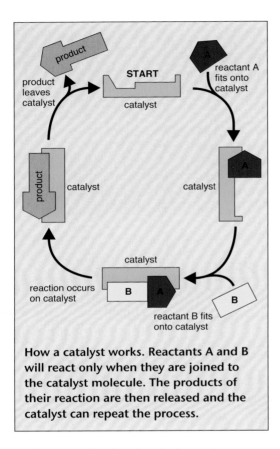

How a catalyst works. Reactants A and B will react only when they are joined to the catalyst molecule. The products of their reaction are then released and the catalyst can repeat the process.

An example of a chemical reaction speeded up using a catalyst is found in fuel cells for spacecraft:

hydrogen + oxygen $\rightarrow$ water

$$2 H_2 + O_2 \rightarrow 2 H_2O$$

This very basic reaction is important for two reasons. It makes water, a vital product that keeps people alive, and it is exothermic—the reaction releases energy that can be put to use. It needs a special catalyst, however, made from the precious metal platinum to make it happen.

This reaction is the basis of the fuel cell in manned space missions. The energy released is used to generate electricity to power the spacecraft while the astronauts use the water for washing, drinking, and mixing with their dried food.

In the chemical industry, nine out of ten chemical products are made with the help of catalysts. These products include **plastics**, fertilizers, medicines, gas, and artificial fibers for clothing. Natural catalysts, called **enzymes,** speed up reactions inside living cells.

Enzymes

Enzymes are natural catalysts produced in your body and in the bodies of most living things. Their job is to speed up vital chemical processes.

When you eat, for example, enzymes from different parts of your digestive system—your mouth, stomach, intestine, liver, and other organs—mix with your food. Each enzyme molecule wraps around a food molecule, separating it into simpler substances. These substances are then dissolved into the bloodstream.

The enzymes in laundry detergents work in a similar way. They break the chemical bonds that hold the proteins in dirt and stains together. Then these proteins can dissolve in water, so they can be washed away.

The problem with enzymes, of course, is that they don't always work to help us! What we call food spoiling is simply the result of microbes that are present on, in, or around the food, producing enzymes that start to digest the food chemicals so that the microbes can feed off them. Microbes are the cause of decomposition and decay.

Enzymes are involved, for example, when an apple turns brown after being cut or bruised. The enzyme is stored inside the apple cells. When the apple is cut, the enzyme is exposed and reacts with oxygen in the air. If the apple is bruised, the enzyme is exposed to air inside the apple. In either case, the enzyme-oxygen reaction turns the fruit brown.

Some familiar foods depend on microbes and their enzymes to break down food. Cheese, yogurt, bread, wine, and beer are created when bacteria and fungi produce enzymes that break down starches, sugar, or milk and give these foods their flavor.

Rotting apples show that enzymes are at work, breaking down the sugars in the apple to feed the growing bacteria and fungi.

Did You Know?

REACTIONS WITH LIGHT AND SOUND
Not all exothermic reactions give out their energy as heat. When someone sets off fireworks, the reaction doesn't just give out heat. It gives out a bright light and a loud bang. Energy can take several forms.

ROBERT H. GRUBBS—DISCOVERER OF NEW WAYS TO "BUILD" MOLECULES USING CATALYSTS

American Robert H. Grubbs (b. 1942) is an organic chemist, which means he studies the chemistry of compounds that contain carbon, especially those compounds found in living things. His work on catalysts won the 2005 Nobel Prize in chemistry. Grubbs's team at the California Institute of Technology (Caltech), Pasadena, figured out how catalysts can be used to remove certain atoms from a compound and replace them with atoms from another compound. The result is a molecule with specialized properties, which can lead to better drugs for the treatment of disease.

CHAPTER 4

Reactivity and How Fast Reactions Go

To understand chemical reactions, we need to understand individual elements, particularly metals. For centuries, people in both science and industry looked for ways to make pure metals. Pure metals have always been valuable. Some, such as iron and copper, can be used to make useful objects. Others, such as gold and silver, are valuable for their appearance and rarity.

As researchers have discovered, metals that can be made into tools and machines generally have to be extracted from **ores**—mineral deposits found in the Earth. The rare metals, however, seem to occur in their pure metallic forms.

The Reactivity Series

This difference led scientists to experiment with different metals to determine their various properties. From their work, scientists discovered which metals reacted with many different substances and which reacted very rarely, if ever, with anything. Eventually, their findings led to a list called the reactivity series, which arranges chemical elements according to how readily they react. The most reactive are at the top of the list and the least reactive at the bottom.

The importance of the reactivity series is that it helps scientists predict how two metals or metallic compounds

will react to one another. It is a rule of the reactivity series, for example, that a metal near the top of the list will react with air or an acid quicker than a metal below it.

Here's the order of metals in the reactivity series:

potassium   **more reactive**
sodium
calcium
magnesium
aluminum
zinc
iron
lead
copper
mercury
silver
platinum
gold   **less reactive**

The list shows that potassium and sodium, at the top of the list, react violently with air and water. Those at the bottom, like silver and gold, are hardly affected by air. That's why these metals are found more or

Even after thousands of years, this Egyptian gold mask has not reacted with the air.

less in their pure form and why, even when they are centuries old, gold objects look like new.

Chemical Reactions

Metals in the middle of the list, such as zinc, iron, and lead, react slowly with air and water. This fact is important when it comes to knowing how to extract the metal from the rock in which it is found (see Chapter 5) and, when it is pure, deciding what objects can be made from it.

Changing Partners

What would happen if you dipped a copper wire into a solution of silver nitrate and left it for thirty minutes? When you pulled the wire from the solution, you'd see that it was covered with furry-looking crystals of pure silver metal.

How did this happen? It has to do with the positions of copper and silver in the reactivity series. This formula shows what took place:

$$Cu + 2AgNO_3 \rightarrow Cu(NO_3)_2 + 2Ag$$

At the start, the silver was bonded with the nitrate as silver nitrate. However, the nature of copper is to react and form copper nitrate. When you put them together, the silver and copper competed for the nitrate. Copper is more reactive than silver, so it ended up with the nitrate. The silver lost the nitrate, so it became just silver. During the reaction, the silver gradually replaced the copper in the solution. Eventually, the silver ions—no longer a part of silver nitrate—settled on the wire.

Rust . . . and Preventing It!

People who own old cars often complain about rusting problems. What is this brown, flaky material known as rust? Rusting is actually a slow chemical change that takes place when iron reacts with oxygen in the air. Steel is a form of iron combined with carbon, so steel also rusts. The rusting process is also called corrosion because the rust eventually eats away, or corrodes, metal. Rust itself is the compound iron oxide, often written Fe_2O_3.

Once rust starts, it does not stop. As flakes of rust fall off, more iron is exposed to the air, and the rusting process continues underneath and spreads. This is what makes the car's exterior look as if it's rotting! Worse yet, if there is water in the air, that further speeds up the rusting reaction.

A coat of paint or plastic applied to the iron or steel can stop the corrosion. Then, the air can't get to the iron, and rusting won't happen. If the paint or plastic coat gets chipped, however, the exposed surface will start to rust again.

Another way to prevent rust is a process called **galvanizing**. Here, the iron or steel is given a coat of zinc metal, which keeps out both air and water. Because zinc is above iron in the reactivity series, it also reacts faster with oxygen, and forms zinc oxide. This creates a protective layer and prevents further corrosion.

Preventing rust is also a concern in regard to canned food. The cans are coated

Over months and years, the iron in steel will react with oxygen and water in the air to make rust.

with tin as a way to stop the steel from rusting. Although the cans are often called tin cans, there's actually very little tin in the total metal. Even so, the tin coating is enough to prevent corrosion, and it won't poison the food inside, as zinc would.

A different solution to corrosion is to treat the steel in a special way when it is made, by bonding it with other metal atoms that will protect it from oxygen. "Stainless steel" is made by adding the metals nickel and chromium to steel. A mixture of metals like this is called an alloy.

Chemical Reactions

The process of galvanization, which adds a layer of less reactive zinc metal, protects these iron farm gates from rusting.

How Fast Do Reactions Go?

All chemical reactions do not take place at the same speed. Explosions are very fast reactions. Most reactions happen more slowly. Bread dough, for example, takes several hours to rise; a car might take months or even years to rust. How long it takes for a reaction to happen depends on how easily the particles of the reactants can get together.

We often speed up or slow down reactions to suit our needs. For example, refrigerating milk slows the rate at which it sours. And, sometimes, it's necessary to make reactions go faster, say, to reduce the cost of production or shorten the time before a new drug is available to doctors Several conditions can affect the speed of a reaction. The most important are:

- temperature
- concentration
- pressure
- surface area

Temperature

You read earlier that activation energy—often in the form of heat—is needed to get a reaction started. Most reactions happen more quickly at higher temperatures. For example, in breadmaking, if you don't warm the yeast, sugar, and flour mixture, the yeast won't grow and produce carbon dioxide, and the dough won't rise.

As the temperature rises, the molecules that take part in the reaction get more energy and move faster. By moving faster, they are more likely to bump into other molecules and so start reacting. At very low temperatures, the molecules are moving so slowly that they don't get close enough to others to react.

The low temperature inside a refrigerator slows down chemical reactions, such as the process of decay.

Concentration

The concentration of a solution is a measure of how many particles there are of it in a certain space, or volume. So, for example, a solution that contains colored dye will be twice as concentrated as another if it contains twice as many dye molecules in the same volume of liquid.

As with temperature, it's a question of making it more likely that the reacting chemicals will come into contact with each other. In a more concentrated solution, it's more likely that reacting molecules will meet and so increase the speed of the reaction. If the solution is less concentrated, fewer molecules will be available to make contact, and the reaction will be slower.

Pressure

Reactions that involve gases are often carried out under pressure because the molecules of a gas are relatively far apart and so would rarely meet to start a reaction. Squeezing them together under high pressure, however, forces them into a smaller space and increases the chance of them reacting.

The gas ammonia is an important raw material in the fertilizer industry. It is made commercially by causing two other gases—nitrogen and hydrogen—to react together. To force them to react, they are put into a tank under a pressure 250 times greater than the normal atmosphere! Then they are heated to

Chemical Reactions

850°F (454°C) to make the reaction go as fast as it possibly can.

Surface Area

The surface area of an object is the amount of surface on the outside. If you want to fry a potato, it would take far less time to fry the potato if you chop it into thin pieces than if you leave it whole. When the potato is chopped up, more of it is in contact with the hot oil then when it is unchopped.

Scientists studying coal mine explosions decided that the most dangerous conditions exist when there is fine coal dust in the air. Coal dust particles are tiny, but they expose far more surface area than a solid wall of coal. With a spark, the wall of coal would not react fast enough with the air to burn, but air filled with coal dust would. There would be an immediate explosion. The greater the amount of coal dust floating in the air, the greater the overall surface area of particles in contact with oxygen. Under these conditions, the slightest spark creates a risk of explosion.

A potato chopped up into long, thin fries will cook a lot quicker than a whole potato fried in the hot fat. That is because the hot oil is in contact with a greater surface area of the potato.

INHIBITORS

Sometimes, chemists want to slow down the speed of a reaction, not speed it up! **Inhibitors** are substances that slow reactions or even stop them from happening completely. Inhibitors make reactions more controllable.

For example, Alfred Nobel, the scientist who invented dynamite, wanted to find a safe way to store nitroglycerin, a highly explosive liquid. Just a slight shaking of a bottle of nitroglycerin could give it enough activation energy to explode! Nobel tried making containers of such things as wood pulp before discovering a special sort of clay that could absorb the explosive safely without reacting with it.

MELVIN CALVIN (1911–1997)—CHEMIST WHO FOLLOWED THE PATH OF CARBON DURING PHOTOSYNTHESIS

Melvin Calvin, co-winner of the Nobel Prize

The American chemist Melvin Calvin was born in Minnesota in 1911. He became a researcher at the University of California–Berkeley in 1937 and eventually became a professor of chemistry there. In 1961, he won a Nobel Prize in chemistry for his work on the reactions of photosynthesis.

Using radioactive carbon, Calvin and his team mapped the path of carbon through a plant during photosynthesis, from its absorption as carbon dioxide through to its conversion into sugars. Calvin's experiments showed that sunlight acts on the green chlorophyll in a plant to fuel the manufacture of compounds.

Chemicals from the Earth

Imagine life without plastics, metals, glass, or concrete. We would find life very difficult if we could only use materials that come from plants and animals. So much of the world around us is made from substances taken from the rocks and minerals below our feet or below the seabed.

ATOMS AND STARS

"One of the wonders of this world is that objects so small can have such consequences: Any visible lump of matter— even the merest speck—contains more atoms than there are stars in our galaxy."

P. W. Atkins, lecturer in physical chemistry, Oxford, England.

Chemicals from Rocks

Rocks are made of one or more salts we call minerals, and it is from these that we obtain many useful materials. Rock salt, for example, is the natural form of sodium chloride. Meanwhile, metals, including copper and aluminum, are all chemically combined in compounds that have to be separated from their ores—the rocks that contain compounds of those metals.

Rock Salt

There are ten major salt deposits in the continental United States. The cities of Cleveland and Detroit are built over huge amounts of rock salt. The salt is mined and spread on the roads in wintertime. Rock salt (also called halite) helps keep the road from freezing by lowering the freezing/melting point of water and turning snow and ice to slush. It works in temperatures down to 15°Fahrenheit (-9.5°Celsius).

Salt deposits are mined by drilling wells down into the salt layer and pumping hot water down the pipe to dissolve the salt. When the water contains as much dissolved salt as it can hold (the saltwater solution is **saturated**), the dissolved salt solution is pumped out. When the water is evaporated from the solution, what's left is mostly sodium chloride.

In many regions, inland lakes are rich in salt, especially in the southwestern United States. Among these is the Great Salt Lake

The Great Salt Lake, Utah. Salt is deposited at the edge of the lake as the water evaporates.

of Utah. As the water evaporates, chunks of salt crystallize on the shore. Many of these inland lakes have already dried up completely, leaving enormous salt deposits that are commercially mined. Examples of this include Searles Lake, California (in the Mojave Desert), Utah's Bonneville Salt Flats, and California's Salton Sea.

Three important chemicals are produced from salt:

Chlorine: used to make plastics and dry-cleaning solvents and to purify water.

Sodium carbonate: used to make glass and colored dyes and as an additive in food and drink.

Sodium hydroxide: also called caustic soda, used to make soap, detergents, synthetic fabrics, and other chemicals.

Chemical Reactions

Copper

Copper is important because it is such a good **conductor** of electricity, so it is used in electric wiring, light fittings, and plug sockets. It is extracted from an ore that contains a mixture of copper, iron, and sulfur. This ore contains as little as 0.5–1 percent of copper metal—the rest is simple rock.

Hot air is blown into a furnace to separate the copper from the iron and the sulfur. The iron and sulfur react with oxygen in the air to make iron oxide and sulfur dioxide. That leaves copper metal that is 98 percent pure, but not pure enough for electrical fittings. To make it

Arizona's copper mines produce two-thirds of the United States's copper.

pure enough for electrical use, the copper has to be purified further using a process called **electrolysis**.

Making copper pure by electrolysis involves a chemical change. This change is caused by passing an electric current through a bath of copper sulfate and sulfuric acid. The current passes between two electrodes dipped in the solution. One of the electrodes, called the cathode, is connected to the negative side of the power supply. The positive electrode, or anode, is a slab of impure copper. Since copper ions are positive (as are all metal ions), they are attracted to the negative cathode. They collect there as a layer of pure copper.

Aluminum

Aluminum is the third most abundant element in Earth's crust after oxygen and silicon. It is made from an ore called bauxite, which is mined in the Caribbean, South America, China, Australia, and Africa.

Sodium hydroxide, a strong alkali, is used to remove silica and iron oxide impurities from the bauxite. This leaves behind aluminum oxide, or alumina. Alumina doesn't dissolve in water, and its melting point is very high, but it will dissolve in a different molten (melted) compound with a lower melting point: sodium aluminum fluoride. The heat needed to keep the mixture molten comes from passing a huge electric current through a container of the mixture.

Once the alumina is dissolved, it separates from its impurities and sinks to the bottom of the vessel, where it collects around the carbon cathode. At the same time, the oxygen in the alumina travels to the positive anode and becomes oxygen gas.

These days, aluminum is largely recycled from cans and other objects containing the metal. This is cheaper than extracting it from its ore. Recycling aluminum saves 95 percent of the energy used to make it new.

Alloys

About six thousand years ago, people discovered that they could make copper harder if they mixed it with tin while both metals were molten. This "metal mixture" is called an alloy, and the alloy of copper and

Aircraft engines and bodies are often made from alloys of aluminum with other metals. The other metals add strength, and the lightness of aluminum reduces weight and, therefore, fuel consumption.

Chemical Reactions

tin is bronze. By changing the amounts of metals in the mixture, the properties of the alloy can be changed.

Alloys are often made to combine several useful properties such as strength and weight. For example, aluminum, magnesium, and copper are combined to make an alloy that is used to build jet aircraft bodies. This means that a lightweight jet plane can stand up to the forces of high speeds and fast turns.

You might have fillings in your teeth. Usually, these have been made from an alloy of five metals—mercury, silver, tin, zinc, and copper—called **amalgam**. When it is molten, amalgam is soft enough to mold into the shape of the cavity before it hardens as a solid filling.

Amalgam fillings are less popular than they once were. Less expensive materials have become available that are both similar in color to real teeth and easier to use.

Plastics

Each year, the world's chemical industry produces about 82 million tons (74 million tonnes) of the gas ethene, also known as ethylene, from oil and natural gas. Ethene reacts easily with many other chemicals, including itself, to produce a range of materials called plastics, including "polythene."

A plastic is a material that can be easily shaped or molded by heat or pressure. In some situations, plastics have replaced materials such as wood, paper, glass, and metal. They are now used in toys, clothes, tableware, paints, packaging, and even furniture.

Most plastics are **polymers**, which means their molecules are made up of thousands of smaller identical units, called **monomers**, joined together. Polymers differ in how they behave when you heat them.

Plastic objects are made in several stages. First, monomers in the form of gases or

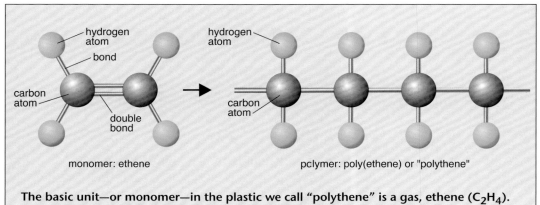

monomer: ethene

polymer: poly(ethene) or "polythene"

The basic unit—or monomer—in the plastic we call "polythene" is a gas, ethene (C_2H_4). Lots of ethene molecules react together to make a long chain, called a polymer.

liquids are heated with a catalyst to speed up the process of polymer formation ("**polymerization**"). The result is a plastic that looks like pellets or a powder. Then the polymers are melted and, depending on the object being made, squeezed,

We use plastic objects in many areas of modern life.

stretched, rolled, or injected. Some are blown, using hot air, into molds to make items such as plastic bottles and containers.

Did You Know

CERAMICS
By adding different compounds to clay and then heating, or firing, the mixture, we can make very tough materials called ceramics. Ceramics are being used to make ball-and-socket hip joints to replace worn-out human hips.

acid compound containing hydrogen, which splits up in water to give hydrogen ions

activation energy the amount of energy needed to make a reaction happen

alkalis bases that dissolve in water

alloy a mixture of two or more metals, or a metal and a nonmetal. Bronze is an alloy of copper and tin.

amalgam a material used for filling teeth, usually made from an alloy of five metals—mercury, silver, tin, zinc, and copper

atom the smallest part of an element. It consists of a nucleus containing protons and neutrons surrounded by orbiting electrons.

bain-marie a pan of hot water into which another bowl containing food is placed, in order to cook or heat the food gently

base a compound that reacts with an acid to give water and a salt. A soluble base is called an alkali.

boiling point the temperature at which a liquid boils

booms a temporary floating barrier used to contain an oil spill

catalyst a substance that speeds up a chemical reaction without being changed itself

caustic harmful; able to damage through chemical reaction

chemical change a change that produces one or more new substances

chromatography a method of separating a mixture into its parts by absorbing them in a material such as filter paper. Different substances in the mixture move through the material at different speeds.

compound a substance containing the atoms of two or more elements

condensation the physical change of a gas or vapor into a liquid

conductor a substance that conducts heat or electricity

crude oil the oil that is taken out of the ground, before it has been refined

diabetes an illness in which people have too much sugar in their blood

distillation a process in which a liquid is boiled and then condensed. It is used to separate mixtures of liquids.

electrolysis a chemical change caused by passing an electric current through a solution or a mixture of substances

electron a negatively-charged subatomic particle. Electrons orbit the nucleus of an atom, whirling rapidly.

element a substance that cannot be broken down further into simpler substances by a chemical reaction

endothermic a chemical reaction in which heat is absorbed from the surroundings

enzyme a catalyst produced by living things to speed up a chemical reaction

evaporation the physical change from a liquid to a vapor. This change takes place at the liquid's surface.

exothermic a chemical reaction in which heat is produced

formula a kind of code or set of symbols made up of letters and numbers that shows what elements make up a substance

fossil fuels fuels that formed over millions of years from the remains of plants or animals

fractional distillation a process used to separate soluble liquids from one another

galvanize to give iron or steel a coat of zinc metal to keep out air and water

indicator a substance that shows the pH of a solution by its change of color, e.g. litmus, universal indicator

inhibitor substances that slow down reactions or keep them from happening. They make reactions more controllable.

insoluble a substance that won't dissolve in a liquid

ion an atom or group of atoms that has lost or gained one or more electrons to become electrically charged

mixture a substance that contains two or more elements or compounds mixed together, which are not chemically combined

molecule the smallest unit of an element or compound. A molecule consists of at least two atoms.

monomer a molecule that is the building block of the polymer

neutralization a process of making an acid or an alkali into a neutral solution

neutrons particles in the center of an atom that have no charge

nucleus the central part of an atom, made up of protons and neutrons. The number of protons is the atomic number of the element.

ore a naturally occurring rock from which metals are extracted

pH a measure of the acidity or alkalinity of a solution. The pH scale extends from 0 to 14. An acidic solution has a pH below 7, a neutral solution has a pH of 7 and an alkaline (or basic) solution has a pH between 7 and 14.

physical change a reversible change of state of a substance, which does not produce any new substances

plastic a compound produced by chemically joining together smaller molecules, usually obtained from oil or natural gas, to make longer ones, which can be shaped to make useful objects

polymer a compound in which the molecules are made up of thousands of smaller identical units

polymerization the process of joining together shorter molecules to make very long ones

protons the positively charged particles in the center of an atom

respiration the process in which oxygen is taken in by living things and used to break down food and make energy

salt a compound formed from the reaction between an acid and a base

saturated having the maximum amount of a substance dissolved in the liquid

soluble a substance that will dissolve in a liquid to form a solution

solute solids dissolved in a solution

solvent the liquid part of a solution; substance into which another substance dissolves

valve the part of a pipe that controls the flow of a gas or liquid

Books

Chahrour, Janet Parks.
Flash! Bang! Pop! Fizz!: Exciting Science for Curious Minds.
Barron's Educational Series, 1st Edition, 2005.

Keller, Rebecca W.
Real Science-4-Kids Chemistry.
Real Science 4 Kids (series)
Gravitas Publications, 2005

Potter, Jean.
Science in Seconds with Toys: Over 100 Experiments You Can Do in Ten Minutes or Less.
San Francisco: Jossey-Bass, 1998.

Ryan, Lawrie.
Chemistry for You.
For You (series)
Nelson Thornes, 2001.

VanCleave, Janice.
Janice VanCleave's Chemistry for Every Kid: 101 Easy Experiments That Really Work
San Francisco: Jossey-Bass, 1989

Web sites

BBC Bitesize
Science: Chemistry
www.bbc.co.uk/schools/ks3bitesize/sci-
ence/chemistry/index.shtml
The BBC's chemistry Web site for eleven-
to fourteen-year-olds.

Chemistry.org
www.chemistry.org/portal/a/c/s/1/acsdis-
play.html?DOC=kids\index.html
The Web site of the American Chemical
Society. Lots of information about chemistry
and its applications in everyday life for children of all ages, plus parents and teachers.

Origins of the Element Names
homepage.mac.com/dtrapp/Elements/celes-
tial.html
This site features elements named after
celestial objects

Rader's Chem4Kids
www.chem4kids.com
An easy-to-read introduction to chemistry,
with quizzes and activities.

What Is Acid Rain
pubs.usgs.gov/gip/acidrain/2.html
A clear explanation of acid rain.

Publisher's note to educators and parents: Our editors have carefully
reviewed these Web sites to ensure that they are suitable for children.
Many Web sites change frequently, however, and we cannot guarantee that
a site's future contents will continue to meet our high standards of quality
and educational value. Be advised that children should be closely supervised
whenever they access the Internet.

INDEX

acid precipitation, 17, 18, 20, 23
acid rain, 17, 18, 20, 23
acids, 14, 15, 16, 17, 18, 19, 20, 21, 22, 23
activation energy, 24, 25
alkalis, 14, 15, 16, 17, 22, 41
alloys, 8, 33, 41, 42
aluminum, 41
amalgam, 42
Atkins, P.W., 7, 38
atoms, 6, 7

bain-marie, 13
bases, 14, 15, 16, 18, 19
bauxite, 41
boiling, 4

Calvin, Melvin, 37
carbonates, 20, 21
catalysts, 15, 27, 28, 29, 43
ceramics, 43
Chopra, Deepak, 20
chromatography, 12, 13
compounds, 8, 9
concentration, 35
condensers, 11
conductivity, 8
conservation of matter, 21
copper, 40, 41
crude oil, 12

decanting, 10
Democritus, 6
diabetes, 13
distillation, 11, 12

electric charge, 6, 7
electricity, 28, 40, 41
electrolysis, 40
electrons, 6, 7
elements, 4, 8, 30, 31
endothermic reaction, 24, 25, 26
energy, 4, 24, 25, 26, 27, 28, 29

enzymes, 28, 29
evaporation, 10, 11, 38, 39
exothermic reactions, 25, 26, 27, 29
explosions, 36

factories, 4
filtering, 10
fireworks, 4
fossil fuels, 17
fractional distillation, 12

galvanizing, 32, 34
gases, 10, 11, 13
gasoline, 4
Grubbs, Robert, H, 29

Harvey, Harold, 23
heating, 8, 24, 25, 34, 35, 36, 40, 41
Hebraea, Mary, 13

ice, 4
indicators, 15, 16
inhibitors, 37
ions, 8, 9, 16, 40, 41

Jung, Carl Gustav, 27

Lavoisier, Antoine, 21
liquids, 4, 10, 11, 12, 13
litmus paper, 16

metals, 8, 14, 18, 30, 31, 32, 33, 34, 38, 40, 41, 42
methane, 26
mixtures, 4, 8, 9, 10, 11
molecules, 6, 7, 8, 9, 18, 20, 21
monomers, 42

neutralization, 81, 19, 22
neutrons, 6, 7
Nobel prizes, 29, 37
Nobel, Alfred, 37
nucleus, 6, 7

ores, 40, 41

particles, 6, 7
pH scale, 16, 17
photosynthesis, 37
plastics, 28, 38, 42, 43
polymers, 42, 43
pressure, 35
protons, 6, 7

reactivity, 8, 30, 31, 32, 33, 34, 35
reactivity series, 30, 31, 32, 34
recycling, 41
refineries, 12
refrigeration, 34, 35
respiration, 27
rock salts, 38, 39
rusting, 5, 32, 33

salt mines, 38, 39
salts, 9, 10, 11, 18, 19, 20, 21
saturated solutions, 38, 39
separating, 10, 11, 12, 13
Sharpless, Barry, 5
solids, 10, 11
solubility, 9, 10
stainless steel, 33
states, 4
surface area, 36

temperature, 35
tooth decay, 23

universal indicators, 16, 17

Wright, Stephen, 34

zeolite, 27